Chaotic Redundancy

Michael Walters

BookLeaf Publishing

India | USA | UK

Presentation by *BookLeaf Publishing*

Web: www.bookleafpub.com

E-mail: info@bookleafpub.com

ISBN: 9789363316799

First edition 2024

This is for any & everyone.

Regardless of circumstance, up bringing, hardship, darkness, etc there is always light.

I am here. I am living proof.

You are here. What will you do next ?

ACKNOWLEDGEMENT

Thank you for being here in this moment. Wherever and whoever you have been, are, & will be..

I am grateful for you, you are appreciated, and you matter.

PREFACE

Let the nonsense commence.

The Grotto

Through all this pain
I remain
I'm curious
What's my purpose
Is there meaning in me
My own thoughts cave in
Trapped in time
Darkness consumes me
Falling behind
At the end of the line
Im fine
Repeats itself
Sins hit as broken stalactites
Mental health sinkhole
The places my mind goes
Aquifer rising
Clock keeps ticking
The walls closing in
How can this be
Will I ever be free

The Chase

Constant suppression
Deep rooted depression
Couldn't prepare
Thinking my thoughts were rare
Leaning over the vanity
Overdosing on my sanity
The days I wanted to detox
Felt like a mental beatbox
The only fix to this
Is permanently missing it
Craving the lift lately
Fighting urges daily
Unaware to where it began
Shame on me
When can it end

The Lonesome

3

On the path less wandered
Growing calluses from within
Struggles aren't seen til well after they begin
Agony crept the lone wolf
Self sabotage is real
Direction unclear
Everyday battles
Fighting the fear
Overcoming uncertainty
The sun starts to rise
One foot in front of the other
Darkness subsides

The Rodin

Is living
The waves cruising into shore
On top of a mountain
Gazing upon the stars
The times we lose ourselves
Searching for meaning
What is living
If we've drifted afar
Money, greed, politics
Sculpting the masses
Media I wonder
Is it all true
Starting with a quill and ink
To losing the right to think

The Aspiration

5

As the sun rises
Darkness fades
Bringing light
Into what was shade
Clouds resting on the horizon
Hills rolling beyond
It's the simplicity
In which I am fond
Bonded by uncertainty
Of what life will bring
Strutting forward
Chasing these dreams

The Boundary

Limits prevent gain
Endure the pain
It's where objectives are made
The chorus will sway one's
Casual beliefs
Skeptics are a relief
Don't be shamed
From orchestrated blame
Not that it should fade
Nor keep from being replayed
A world drenched in loathing
Consensus exploding
It seems so brutal
With outcomes constantly futile

The Purity

Days move forward
Even when we're held back
Anxiety can creep
Bring us down
Yet the earth continues
Spinning around
Life isn't easy
It hurts us all
Determination & grit
Doesn't weather the falls
Keep in tact what's fact
What's true
What matters to you
Should always be pure

The Uncovering

The fog acts as a shield
Rolling across the valleys
Blinding the light
Sinister rally
Confusion sets in
Hints of despair
Pondering what could possibly prevail
It begins its demise
Boasting the size of what is still there
Taking in the open air
All doubt restrained
With what once was vain
Clouded judgement has lapsed
Another day to claim

The Alarm

Many days have passed
Than could be savored
Let go of what once was
From all the favors
Underlying the popularity
Comes mass unfamiliarity
Loss of clarity
Beginning the path
Some would say wrath
Some would say reckoning
A calmer tone
Consists of
Personal awakening

The Plausibility

As high as the mountains peak
Low as the earthworm seeks
The keys of nature
Play a special tone
Solidarity can impose
By the thrust alone
Hesitation can nullify
Simple discretion
As the Cards dealt
Don't guarantee succession

The Tenseness

Storms will brew
There's purpose
There's meaning
Beyond the midst of rain
Uncanny as it seems
Thunder and lightening
Have a balance they bring
The scathe of any storm
Dereliction paths
One can roam
Without scorn
Foreign examination
Can yield elucidation

The Unfolding

I used to reminisce
The cold
And Debated the fold
At times
I didn't like the hand I was delt
Til the day
Your warmth was felt
Suddenly as you may turn to me
I know it's where I wanna be
the preciousness of your voice
Leaves me no choice
I'm always stuck
like glue - starring at you

The Indisposition

Gloating and jealousy
Reek from beyond
This is only how far we've come
Decency is lost between all these people
Shouting and cursing from a position that's fetal
Giving in to what's easy
Hopelessness, addiction, any affliction
Unbeknownst to those who
Think they're alright
Nothing is darker than internal fight

The Dedication

The tenderness of
every single kiss
lost in bliss
I want every bit of this
The good, The bad, The rough
Even when times are tough
Your Stubbornness is no joke
You can Push and poke
It Still won't be enough
For me to revoke

The Misunderstood

15

Flirting turns to hurting
Intentions impure
Insecurities, impatient,
Doesn't mean your not great
Open your eyes
Let's hypothesize
Go to a dream state
Start to facilitate
What matters to you
Can always be true

The Vow

I wont refrain
to go through Any pain
Hypothetical no longer
I yearn to grow stronger
Still falling everyday for you
Knowing your hearts so pure
I vow to always be true to you

The Cost

Questioning the rate
Of meeting the fate
When time stands still
Questioning how to feel
Should I be doing this
Is the fix worth the risk
Even though it's not
It's already been bought
Here in my hand
It's time to begin
A slow burn of regret
Until needs are met
The path my mind took
Moving as a rook
This way or that way
Gambling life away
Treacherous game to play
Extraordinary price to pay
What's it worth to you
To finally be through

The Bottom

Ending up an outcast
Questioning the past
Reconvening the pieces
Shattered along the way
Hoping for a day
There won't be a price to pay
When are the dues fulfilled
And this heart won't yield

The Weight

Once upon of time
Wanting to feel alive
All these demons inside
Darkness consuming
As the depths of the sea
Struggling to breathe
Intrusive thoughts drowning me
No sense of who'd I'd be
Weight of the world
Smothering thee

The Question

Gazing beyond appearance
Feeling what's in a soul
Sense of understanding
Even between foes
In a world left squandered
Do I want this any more
Is it worth living
If what for is unknown

The Euolgy

Harmonious epiphanies
Yet nothing left in me
Stuck feeling behind
Whirlwind in my mind
Strayed sense of time
Heart beating on a straight line
Is it worth moving forward
Only to hurt again
Earned these scars
Each along the way
Might not have seized anything
Yet applied myself today
Is that enough
Too eventually relieve this pain
Does it matter when
I feel this self gain